Unique Baby Names Meanings

Beautiful and Unusual Baby Names That Will Make Your Child Special (Full Edition)

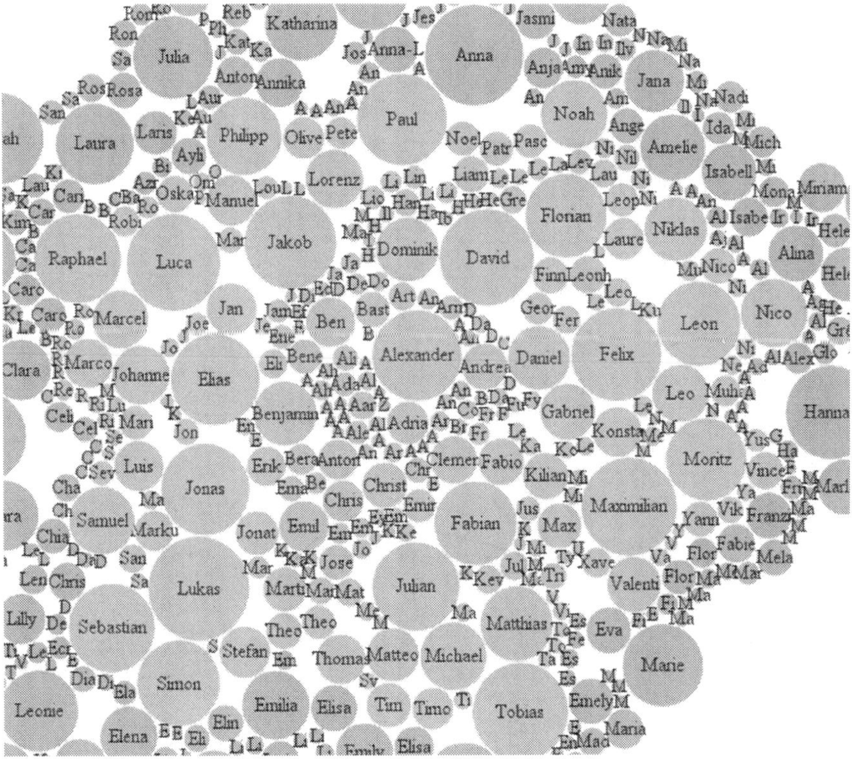

Table of Contents

Introduction 3

Chapter 1 – Children With Unique Names In Our Society 4

Chapter 2 – Methods For Selecting A Name For Your Baby ... 8

Chapter 3 – Top-20 Perfect and Original Names For Girls 12

Chapter 4 – Top-20 Perfect and Original Names For Boys ... 16

Chapter 5 – Unique and Beautiful Unisex Names 19

Chapter 6 – Unique And Meaningful Names For Boys 22

Chapter 7 – Unique and Meaningful Names For Girls 48

Chapter 8 – The Most Beautiful Names Around The World ... 76

Chapter 9 – Common Names To Avoid 83

Conclusion 86

Introduction

What's there in a name?

Well, the answer is everything. We are known by our name. As we grow up, it becomes a part of our identity and reflects our nature in more ways than one can imagine. Not only we are known by our name to our friends and family, but this is how we are remembered by everyone around us. A name is a deal-breaker and can either make or break your child's confidence.

If you are expecting a baby and haven't picked a perfect name for your little one, then you have certainly come to the right place. Don't follow the crowd and name your kid a forgettable name. Instead, do some research and give your little one the best present of their life – an unforgettable name.

Too often, we make the mistake of following the ongoing trend and pick a common name for our kids. It might seem unique, but in the long haul, it can cause more damage to your kid in a disastrous way. It has been observed that kids are bullied on the basis of their names. If your little one has a unique or the kind of name that can easily be compared to a funny thing, the chances are that they could be an obvious target of bullies.

To make sure that they have a happy and nurturing childhood, it is of utmost importance to give them a name that can make them feel proud of themselves. In the long haul, all of us reflect the meaning of our name. If you want your kid to be successful and make their own path, then think of a positive name that will act as a perfect inspiration for them.Here in this informative guide, we have handpicked some of the best names for both, boys and girls. We have also come up with an interesting way that can help you pick a unique name for your baby. Read on and come up with a meaningful name for your little one. Give them something to be proud of for the rest of their lives!

Chapter 1 – Children With Unique Names In Our Society

Ever wonder why there are a few kids that stand out from the crowd and are able to create their individual space without any effort? Well, it's all because of their names. We all hear some unusual and interesting names now and then that stay with us in the long run. Now, when you are expecting your little one to arrive in your life, why not come up with such an amazing name for them as well!

We have a highly developed society where people from different backgrounds, cultures, and religions entwine together. Our diversity is the key to our growth as we all are able to bring the best out of everything in a unique way. Before we introduce some of the unique and meaningful names that you can give to your little one, let's explore some of the popular names that we absolutely love!

These children are already famous for their names. Let's see what makes it so damn special. You never know, you might end up picking a name from this list!

1. Abel: A biblical name, it certainly goes way back to the origin of our race. The literal meaning of it is "breath" and was the name given to the second child of Adam and Eve. Though, the name became a modern sensation when Amy Poehler gave her son this unique name.

2. Amaya: The most obvious meaning of Amaya is "midnight rain". Not only is the name poetic, it sounds flawless for a girl. Daughter of Mariska Hargitay, the famous Law and Order actress chose this beautiful name for her daughter.

3. Arabella: Not only is this a unique name, but it also sounds pretty royal too! Commonly known as the name of Ivanka

Trumph's daughter, it has certainly come like a breath of fresh air to all the common names we have been hearing these days.

4. Ava: The direct meaning of Ava is "like a bird". The name is not only simple and direct but has a perfect poetic touch to it. Ava is the name of Hugh Jackman's daughter. It was also used by Reese Witherspoon to name her daughter.

5. Aviana: The name came into the spotlight when Amy Adams used it for her daughter. It was assumed that she blended the popular names "Ava" and "Ana" to give birth to such a unique name.

6. Beckett: Originally the last name, it means "dweller near the brook" and became quite popular in the recent times. The interesting name was used by Stella McCartney and Conon O'Brien to name their sons.

7. Bennett: Just like Beckett, this last name has come out as an obvious choice for a lot of people these days. Bennett means "little-blessed one" and has been taken by celebrities like Jane Krakowski to name their baby boy.

8. Charlotte: It is one such name that never goes out of the trend. It might be a little common, but the simplicity of it is something which is adored by a lot of people. Name to a lot of celebrities, it is also the name of the daughter of Marc Mezvinsky and Chelsea Clinton.

9. Fiona: You can't come up with a prettier name for your little angel than this one. The most literal meaning of Fiona is "the one who is fair and beautiful". A perfect feminine name, it was used by Jennie Garth as well to name her daughter.

10. Flynn: This traditional Gaelic name is not just cute, but it will age perfectly with your little boy. Maybe this is why it was picked by Orlando Bloom for his little baby boy.

11. Harper: A unisex name, this one has been around for a long time. We all know the award-winning author Harper Lee, who made it a household name. Though, it has been used by plenty of celebrities as well. Name for the newborn daughter of David and Victoria Beckham, it was also used by Neil Patrick Harris to name one of his adorable twins.

12. Hazel: Though, the name might be a favorite among millenniums after the renowned John Green book, but the beauty of it is certainly can't be overlooked upon. The vintage name originally made a comeback, when Julia Roberts gave one of her twin daughters this beautiful name.

13. Helena: This age-old name tracks back to the Greek mythology. The most literal meaning of it is "shining light or sun rays". Helena is a little twist to the original name Helen, the daughter of Zeus. The name also came in fashion when Kelley Rutherford, the famous Gossip Girl star gave her daughter this legendary name.

14. Julian: This perfect name for a baby boy is not only timeless, but goes all the way back to the Julius Caesar age. A masculine name, it has just the perfect ring to it and will remain a favorite for years. Lisa Kudrow also gave her son this perfect name!

15. Levi: The name is not just simple, but has a raw masculine approach as well. One of the most preferred names for boys, it was also used by Matthew McConaughey to name his son.

16. Nahla: If you want to take the help of a foreign language, then this can be one of the names for your little girl. The Arabic name translates to "the circle of life" and came into the limelight when Halle Berry used this exotic word to name her little princess.

17. Olive: How can someone not love this adorable name, right? Simple yet admirable, it was also used by Isla Fisher to name her daughter back in 2007.

18. Stella: Probably one of the most common yet obvious choices of names, Stella was used by a lot of celebrities including Matt Damon, Ellen Pompeo, Tori Spelling, and more to name their daughter.

19. Zachary: Not only it is a timeless name, but it will also stay unique for a long time. Though the name is a little traditional, but it has a perfect modern ring to it. Maybe, this is why Sir Elton John named his baby boy Zachary and impressed everyone with his traditional choice.

20. Zahara: We all know this famous name, as it came into the spotlight when Angelina Jolie and Brad Pitt named their little girl Zahara. It means "shining" and it certainly goes well with their little one.

When it comes to choices for picking up a name, there is certainly no end to it. You might find a limitless number of unique names for your little one. Though, it is not about picking a different name. It is all about coming up with a name that would not only be interesting, but meaningful as well.

Now when you know about some of the most remarkable names that prevail in our society, it is a time when you learn the basics of coming up with a perfect name. Turn your page as the next chapter will introduce you to some of the finest methods of coming up with an amazing name for your baby.

Chapter 2 – Methods For Selecting A Name For Your Baby

Choosing a name for your little one can sometimes be the toughest task in this world. You might be getting a thousand options in your mind and picking your favorite one can be the hardest thing to do. Your baby's name would be a part of their identity. They would be called by that name for the rest of their lives, and you certainly don't want to give them a chance to object, right?

Thankfully, we have come up with an easy method of selecting an interesting name for your baby. Follow these quick and seamless steps, and by the end, you will have a meaningful name for your little one.

How does it sound?

Always recite the name loudly before reaching a conclusion. There are times when you can come up with an interesting name, but if it doesn't sound good, there is no reason for putting your kid under such a hardship for the rest of their lives. You don't want others to pronounce your baby's name in the wrong way. Needless to say, your kid would be spending their entire life trying to correct others as well.

Combine a prospective name with your last name and make sure that they both are going well with each other. If you have a shorter last name, try to come up with a longer first name and vice-versa. If your last name starts with a vowel, try to refrain yourself from coming up with a name that ends with a vowel, as it might sound like a single name.

Don't try to rhyme the last and the first name together at any cost. This would sound really funny, and your kid might get picked on for no reason.

The degree of uniqueness

A lot of parents think that giving their baby a unique name will solve their dilemma. Though it is always a good idea to name your kid something different, but you should always know how to maintain the degree of uniqueness.

Giving them an extremely unique name that can't be comprehended by anyone would be nothing less than giving your child a lifetime punishment. It would be followed by mispronunciations and unwanted attention. Think of a unique name, but don't go overboard!

A meaningful name

It is always recommended to come up with a name that has a meaning behind it. You should always remember that by giving your child a name, you are giving them the most significant part of their identity. It has been proven that kids reflect the meaning of their name as they grow up. Make sure that you come up with a thoughtful name for your little one. Though, don't make it super tough or complicated for others to understand.

Initials

This is one thing that is forgotten by a lot of parents. Before you give your baby a name, know how their initials are sounding. George Ian Joe might sound an average name, but the initials would end up making your kid a superhero! This might cause unwanted attention in their life and their high school days might end up being disastrous.

Get inspired from family

There is this amazing charm in naming your baby after your beloved father or grandmother, right? It is the best way to pay your loved ones some respect and keep their legacy alive. If you think there is a close family member who has an impressive name, there is no harm is sharing the same as either the first or the middle name for your baby.

Think of the long haul

Come up with a name that will age well with your child. Giving a name like Angel, Bunny, Bucks, or Lucky might seem cute when they are a baby, but think of what will happen when they will age. A 40-year old man with a name like "Lucky" might face a lot of inappropriate and awkward situations.

According to Greek and Hindu mythology, our name signifies who we are. Gradually, as your little one would grow up, they would adapt the meaning of their name and would implement it in their life. A name definitely has a lot more significance in your baby's life than you can think and our suggestions will definitely come handy to you!

Have a look at some of these foolproof suggestions of unique baby names and be inspired to come up with an out-of-the-box name for your little one.

1. Ancient Greek names

Ancient Greek names never go out of trends. Not only they sound significant but have a profound meaning and an enchanting story behind them as well. Even celebrities like Gwen Stefani have named her son Apollo, after the Greek demi-god. You can opt for unique names like Athena, Ares, Augustus, Atlas, Olympia, Orion, Penelope, and a lot more.

2. Herb or nature-related names

If you are a lover of nature, then you certainly can't find a better inspiration for your baby's name that the Mother Nature herself. Why not pick a spice's name like Saffron, Cinnamon, Sage, or Rosemary. You can always pick a plant's name like Aspin, Cedar, or Ciceley.

3. Wildflower names

You can also name your baby girl after your favorite flowers like Rose, Jasmine, Daisy or Lily. Some other wildflower names can also be used like Willow, Daphne, Clover, Azalea, or Zinnia.

4. Season inspired names

This one will definitely get your kid noticed and will be everyone's favorite in no time. A name like Winter, Summer, or Autumn will definitely never go out of season! You can also pick your favorite month like January, March, or April as your baby's name.

If you like a particular season, then you can always explore peculiar characteristics of it. For example, if your baby is born in winter, names like Snow, Frost, or Blue can also be considered.

5. Literary inspired names

There is definitely nothing better than naming your baby after a literary legend. Be inspired by an epic novel and give your little one a legendary name like Atticus, Thiago, Elsa, Aldys, Sawyer, Esme, Olive, Hazel, and more. You can also name your little ones after famous writers like Jane, Kipling, Ernest, or Agatha.

There are thousands of ways for coming up with a unique name for your baby. Just like an artist, you can find inspiration in everything – from Mother Nature to the cosmic world. It might seem a herculean task, but after getting acquainted with the above-mentioned tips, we are sure you can select just a perfect name for your baby. If you are not able to decide that one special name, then don't worry. We have handpicked some of the best names for both boys and girls that can come handy to you!

Chapter 3 – Top-20 Perfect and Original Names For Girls

Planning to name your little angel? Worry not! We have come up with plenty of suggestions to take you out of your dilemma. There is a reason why more people are thinking out-of-the-box and unique names for their babies.

Gone are the days when "Adam" and "Amy" were used to be the obvious choice of names. You don't want your kid to be just another boy or girl out there, with a common name. If you want them to be remembered by everyone, then give them a unique name. This will not only make them stand out from the crowd, but will also make them more confident and proud of their identity.

To make things easier for you, we have handpicked some of the best names for girls. Give your angel a meaningful name that she can be proud of for the rest of her life, by picking one of these unique and thoughtful suggestions.

1. Amor: A traditional Spanish name, not only it would be a perfect feminine choice for a girl's name, it also has an effortless ring to it. Although you might know the meaning behind this perfect name, the Spanish word translates to "love". If you are looking for something simple yet elegant, then Amor would be just the perfect choice.

2. Bryn: These days, it is recommended to choose a simple yet meaningful name to avoid any complications in the future. If you think the same, then you will love this Welsh name. The original meaning of Bryn is "hill" and makes a perfect name for a baby girl. A timeless name, this one would be an obvious choice for all the nature lovers out there.

3. Cara: The word has both Latin as well as Irish origin. A flawless name, it has been in trends since the 1970s and is still considered as a chic choice. It means "beloved" in Latin and has been transformed to other names like Cherie or Carina. Whereas, in Irish, Cara means "friend".

4. Davina: Commonly known as the feminine equivalent of David, the name is still a unique one and is picked by only a few parents, despite its tasteful meaning. It is a name of Scottish origin which means "friend" or "a beloved". Davina is a perfect feminine name that will go timelessly with your little one.

5. Elle: One of the most sophisticated and stylish names of the lot, it has a perfect ring to it and will be everyone's favorite in no time. The word is originally derived from French and translates to "she". One certainly can't come up with a sweeter name than this.

6. Edith: An age-old English name, it is still widely used by parents all over the world. It means "blessed" or "riches". The name is also commonly used in French and Dutch culture, as it has a universal meaning and a perfect sound that will never go out of the style.

7. Felicity: If you are searching for something unique yet meaningful, then Felicity will be a perfect option. Though, the literal meaning of it is "happiness", but it is originally derived from Latin and means "good fortune" or simple "luck". It is also assumed that the name has been derived from Felicitas, the name of the renowned Roman goddess.

8. Gia: One certainly can't go wrong with such a beautiful name. Not only is this name poetic, but it sounds amazing as well. Gia has been originally derived from Latin and means "God's gracious gift". It is assumed that Gia is the feminine counterpart of Giovanni.

9. Iris: One of the most everlasting names, Iris has several meanings. The scientific meaning of Iris is used to depict the colored part of a human eye. Though, the name goes back to the Greek mythology and was given to the Greek goddess of the rainbow. Iris is also a commonly found flower, though its colloquial meaning is often considered as a "rainbow".

10. Lyn: Fierce yet feminine, this simple name surely has a profound meaning. The Welsh baby name translates to "lion-like" and is considered as the feminine version of Leo. Though, the name is quite uncommon and is also translates to a leader.

11. Mia: A simple yet unique name, Mia has an Italian origin and is considered as a shorter version of Maria. Its literal meaning is "mine", which makes it such a keeper.

12. Ophelia: If you are a lover of literature and would like to give a unique name to your girl, then consider her naming Ophelia. The Greek baby name translates to "help" or "the one who help others". The name became quite famous after Shakespeare's Hamlet, in which Ophelia played a vital role.

13. Quinn: The Gaelic baby name is certainly catching up a lot these days. It means "assistance", "help", or "counsel", and would be a perfect name for a baby girl. Feminine and having a perfect sound, it was also a widely used Irish last name.

14. Rei: The name has a Japanese origin and though it is a unisex name, but it is commonly used for girls these days. The Japanese meaning of Rei is "strive" or "related to law". Though, Rei also has a Hebrew connection and is translated to "my shepherd" or "my companion", which makes it such an interesting choice for a name!

15. Tabitha: If you are a little traditional, then give your baby girl this classic Hebrew name, which originally translates to "grace". It is assumed that the word has been originally taken from the Arabic word, Gazelle, which can also make a great name for your baby.

16. Ulyana: One might not come up with a better name for a girl that starts with a "U" than Ulayana. The Russian origin name is certainly making its way to the rest of the world with its sheer beauty and meaning. It translates to "youthful" and has an attractive sound as well!

17. Valentina: One of the most feminine and poetic names of all, Valentina takes its original from the Roman word Valentinus. The original meaning of it is "strong" or "someone who is healthy", which makes the name both beautiful and thoughtful.

18. Violet: You know you have picked a nice name when just the mere mention of it brings a smile to your face. Violet is certainly a name like that. It is unique, meaningful, and most significantly, timeless. We all know Violet as the soothing color or the beautiful flower. Though, it is also assumed that Violet has been derived from Viola, which is a Latin word, and makes a great choice for a name in itself. Viola is the large musical instrument of the violin family and can also be considered to name your little girl.

19. Yasmin: Be inspired by nature and name your little girl after this beautiful flower. The Persian name is equivalent to the English word "Jasmine". Yasmin has a peculiar charm which makes the name so unique.

20. Zara: If you like to pick something outlandish and yet known to everyone, then Zara would be a perfect name. The Arabic name is not only crisp, but has a profound meaning as well. Translates to "princess", the name would be adored by your little angel for the rest of her life.

Those were some fascinating names for sure! Not only did these names sound so amazing, but they had such a profound meaning as well. If you are expecting a baby girl, you can certainly pick one of these beautiful names or can come up something on your own as well. If you still don't know the gender of your unborn child, then don't worry! We have come up with a list of some of the best names for boys as well in the next chapter.

Chapter 4 – Top-20 Perfect and Original Names For Boys

Sometimes, naming a boy can be the hardest thing, right? It might seem a little overwhelming in the beginning with so many options, but after picking your favorite options, it would become a whole lot easier for you! If you are expecting a little boy in your life, then why not come up with a thoughtful name for him. We have handpicked some of the best names for a baby boy. Have a look as they might become your favorite in no time.

1. Asher: Go a little traditional and give your boy this Hebrew name. It originally translates to "happy" or "happiness" and was the same name given to Jacob's 8th son, who was promised a life of contentment. Now, who wouldn't want such a thoughtful gift for their kid!

2. Atlas: The name has multiple meanings. Not only it represents the entire world, but it is also a Greek name, which was given to a Titan. The name has a catchy sound, which will be a favorite among your family and friends in no time.

3. Bane: Not only it sounds so good, the meaning of this name will certainly win your heart over. The Hawaiian origin name translates to "the long-awaited child".

4. Clement: The name needs no introduction. It is shared by fourteen popes and several saints. Needless to say, any child with this name would be a blessed one!

5. Declan: The Irish origin name is translated to "full of goodness", which makes it such an optimistic name!

6. Gale: Short, but probably one of the most lively and fun name that one can think of their baby boy. The original meaning of Gale is the one who is "jovial". Not only is the name so simple, but it has a perfect ring to it as well.

7. Hudson: Simple yet classy, the name is certainly synonymous with royalty and means "the son of the hooded man". It is originated from the German word "hug", which means mind, spirit, or heart.

8. Jagger: The name became quite famous Rolling Stones singer and became a household name. It means "peddler" or "carter" and comes with a unique nickname "jag" that would be everyone's favorite.

9. Kai: The multilingual name has several meanings. Kai is a Hawaiian word which depicts the sea, while the Irish meaning of it is "rejoice". Not only is the name so sweet, but it has such a profound meaning to it as well.

10. Lafayette: Give your little boy a kind of poetic name that would get him noticed, no matter where he goes. The French name is commonly used as a surname as well and has an exotic sound to it.

11. Llam: Simple yet profound, the name is devoted to the one who is a protector and has a strong will-power. Often considered as a short version of William, the name certainly has a perfect ring to it.

12. Marden: The unique name is translated to "a valley with a pool" and would be instantly picked by the lovers of the Mother Nature.

13. Noah: We all have heard of the legendary story of Noah and his ark that saved the entire world. If you want to go traditional, then you certainly can't come up with anything better than this Hebrew name, as it means "comfort" and is synonymous with longevity and peace.

14. Otis: The German origin name means "the one who is wealthy" and is used by a lot of people all over the world for its positive meaning.

15. Payton: This English name would be loved by everyone. It has the original meaning of a "warrior's estate", which symbolizes how royal the name is!

16. Sawyer: The Celtic origin name is certainly unique and will let your boy stand out from the crowd. Translates to "timber", it would be an obvious choice for all the nature lovers out there.

17. Raleigh: The exotic name will let your kid be close to nature. Often considered as something related to a meadow, it is also a commonly found last name.

18. Ranell: The English name means "strong counselor" and would be a perfect choice for a baby boy, considering the uniqueness and the catchy sound of the name.

19. Taren: If you have a boy who is full of life and enthusiasm, why not give him this electrifying name. The Welsh origin name translates to "thunder" and sounds amazing as well!

20. Zachary: The religious name is chosen by a lot of thoughtful parents all over the world. The famous disciple of Jesus, it has a Hebrew origin and dates back to the biblical time. Surprisingly, even today, the name is not so common and has a catchy sound to it.

We are sure you must have loved the above-mentioned suggestions of names for a baby boy. Now you can certainly come up with an interesting name for your little one and move over from all the common choices. Naming a boy can get tricky at times. Think of something different, which would make him stand out from the crowd, but consider the degree of uniqueness. You don't want your son to explain the meaning of his name to others for the rest of his life, right?

If you are still not able to pick that one perfect name for your baby, then don't worry. We have come up with some unique names as well that are unisex in nature. They would definitely be of great help to you. Read on and pick that one perfect name for your little one without any hassle.

Chapter 5 – Unique and Beautiful Unisex Names

There are a lot of parents out there who don't like to reveal the gender of their unborn baby. If you would like to get surprised, then it is high-time you prepare yourself with the best of the both worlds! There is just something about unisex names which makes them so damn interesting. Names like "Amanda" or "Kyle" might come and go, but strong unisex names like "Skylar" or "Tamryn" will always stay in the trends.

If you are still not able to make your decision, then let us suggest you with some of the best unisex names that can be picked by you without any trouble. Take a look and choose your favorites!

1. Adal: It means "noble" and will certainly go well as a unisex name. It has a German origin and is used as a surname as well

2. Bailey: Originally a surname, it has been adapted as a commonly known unisex name by parents these days. It represents someone who enforces the law and supports justice.

3. Brook: Often spelled as "Brooke" as well, the English name means stream and is one of the most interesting unisex names out there.

4. Casey: The name has a Gaelic origin and it means someone who is vigilant or attentive. It is also spelled as "Cacey" by a lot of people.

5. Corey: The Gaelic name is both trendy and thoughtful. It means "hollow dweller" and can be spelled in different ways like "Cory" or "Kori" as per the gender of your baby.

6. Dakota: It means "friendly" and represents someone who could be an ally. Not only the name has a traditional American meaning, but it is largely considered as one of the most positives names for a baby.

7. Damien: The French name means "the one who tames others", which makes it not only a powerful name but a little poetic as well.

8. Eli: This Hebrew name, which means "high" and can go flawlessly with a long surname. The name was used by many priests and saints already, which makes it such a keeper.

9. Farren: A spelling variant, which is making a lot of buzzes these days. The name has an Irish origin and means "the one who love adventures".

10. Hayden: The Greek name has an interesting meaning and sounds amazing as well. It translates to "valley with hay", which makes it such an interesting name.

11. Lane: One can surely not come up with a name so simple yet adorable. A timeless option, it will grow with your little one in the best way. Used to depict a path or a way, it is a new suggestion for a unisex name that is making a lot of buzz these days.

12. Madison: Though the name was originally thought of as a boy name, but it has been rapidly adapted for girls as well, which makes it one of the perfect choices for a unisex name. Not only is the name so simple, it has a thoughtful meaning as well. It commonly translates to "the strong fighter" or "the god's gift".

13. Phoenix: We all know the meaning of this amazing name. If you know your baby has what it takes to carry this powerful name, then there is no harm in giving them this striking name that will certainly get them noticed. The reference of it has been used in several mythological stories as the bird that was burnt and got reborn with its own ashes.

14. Rudy: It can also be considered as a shorter version of Rudolph and can be used as a girl as well as a boy name as well. It means "famous wolf" and has a crisp yet masculine sound to it.

15. Shea: The Irish origin name is now used for both boys and girls. Its literal meaning is "the one who is majestic" and will certainly never go out of the trend.

16. Skylar: The name certainly has a unique sound, which makes it so catchy. Used for both boys and girls, it is mostly related to the sky and depicts the beauty of the Mother Nature.

17. Tamryn: The name not only has a biblical meaning but is a common Russian name as well. It translates to a Palm Tree and can be used for both boys and girls.

18. Taylor: We certainly can't put an end to this list without including this legendary unisex name. Probably one of the most respected and thoughtful unisex names of all, it is still unique and sounds perfect.

19. Valdis: Often known as "the chosen one", this Welsh origin name is not only thoughtful but sounds pretty royal as well.

20. West: If you want to give your baby a different name and yet make it sound awesome, then you should surely consider this option. The direction has a fair meaning and if it means something special to you, then you should definitely not hesitate in naming your little one "West".

From Adal to West, we have suggested plenty of unisex names that are not only interesting but have a profound meaning behind them as well. The thoughtful nature of these names is what makes them so everlasting in nature. If you are still not sure of a name, then move to our next chapter. We have selected a wide range of names for boys and girls that would be of a great help to you. Let's have a look.

Chapter 6 – Unique And Meaningful Names For Boys

If you are expecting a baby boy, then you should definitely handpick some of the most thoughtful names for him. It is always a good idea to be prepared and has a list of a few prospective names than to simply rush and come up with a name at the last moment.

Finding just the right kind of name for a boy can be a tedious task. Don't worry, as we are here to help you. Have a look at these suggestions that would help you pick the perfect name for your little one.

- Arthur: The Victorian name has a timeless charm to it. The name was given to legends like King Arthur. The Shakespearean name was also used in his famous play.

- Anthony: Also appeared in the famous play of "Anthony and Cleopatra", the name has a Latin origin and translates to "the one who is priceless". Needless to say, it has such a thoughtful meaning that can't be missed.

- Andrew: Probably one of the most subtle yet classic names of all. It is linked to someone who is a warrior and literally translates to "manly". It has a Greek origin.

- Alexander: Who can forget the great Emperor Alexander, who once shaped the history of our world? Give your boy this legendary name and inspire him to achieve great heights. Alejandro is another alternative to this name. It means the one who has protected the mankind.

- Aiden: The name has an Irish origin and translates to the one who is fierce and brave. Now, who doesn't want their little boy to have these amazing qualities, right? Also, the name has a certain ring to it.

- August: Be inspired from the name of the month and give your boy this unique name. It has a Latin origin and is named after the great Roman god.

- Ace: The one who is superior to others or who excels in everything he does. Ace is such a crisp yet meaningful English-origin name.

- Adonis: In Greek Mythology, Adonis was known as one of the most handsome men of all. The lover of Aphrodite, the name would certainly make your boy stand out.

- Andres: The poetic name translates to the one who is brave and charismatic. It has a Spanish origin.

- Axel: The Danish origin name means the protector or father of peace and serenity.

- Ari: Short yet meaningful, Ari has a Hebrew origin and translates to a lion or lion-like.

- Amare: Amare is certainly a unique name for a boy. It means the one who is exotic, lively, and wanted by everyone else. Not just the meaning, the mere pronunciation of the name is so unique. This one should definitely be on your list.

- Alfonso: Used by more than 20 kings of Europe, Alfonso is a name that oozes out royalty in each and every bit of it.

- Arlo: The name has a Spanish origin and means a "berry tree". It has a vintage feel to it that makes it such a hit.

- Aaric: The Norse-origin name can be a great alternative to Eric or Arrik.

- Achilles: If you have a thing for Greek mythology, then you and your loved ones are going to adore Achilles is well. The legendary warrior played a major role in the Trojan War.

- Acis: Another Greek name, he was the famous Nymph and the son of Galatea.

- Adahy: The Native American name means someone who lives in the woods or has been originated in it.

- Actaeon: The Latin name has plenty of mythological tales associated with it and translates to "a stag".

- Addis: The Biblical name is gaining its charm. It was the name given to the son of Adam.

- Adib: The one who is cultured, polite, and honest. Parents also choose "Adab" as its alternative.

- Aeolus: The name certainly has a unique spelling and pronunciation. The work has a Latin origin to it and means the one who is the keeper of the winds.

- Aharon: The Egyptian name is not at all a common one and means the one who is praised and exalted.

- Ahren: The German name literally translates to "Eagle". Needless to say, it would be aptly chosen by every patriotic American.

- Aja: The Hindu-origin name has a majestic meaning. It translates to the one who is not born or can't be destroyed.

- Albus: The character appeared in the Harry Potter series and became an instant hit among all the fans. It means the one who is white.

- Alistair: The name is given to the one who likes to defend the mankind and humanity.

- Amias: The one who loves the God.

- Amery: The German name means the one who is divine and pious.

- Ammar: The Arabic name translates to the man who likes to create new things.

- Amon: The highly renowned name given to the immortal Egyptian god.

- Amycus: The Greek word traces back in time as it was the name given to the son of Poseidon.

- Beau: The name is still not that popular and translates to the one who is loved. It has a peculiar Southern charm that makes it such a hit.

- Brent: The name has a Celtic origin and means the top of the hill.

- Brendan: The royal name translates to "prince". It has a Celtic-Greek origin to it.

- Baron: The name has multiple meanings. In French, it means the one who is noble while the English meaning of it means a warrior.

- Bryson: The name has gained a wide popularity recently. It means the son of Brice and is associated with contentment and happiness.

- Brawley: A simple yet thoughtful English name. It is the part of the meadow that goes to the slope of the hill. If you are a nature-lover, then you should certainly include this in your list.

- Bain: The one who likes to live nearby a stream or being surrounded by nature. It has a Gaelic origin to it.

- Badden: The Welsh name translates to "a boar".

- Baen: The Scottish name is given to babies who have a flawless skin.

- Barrin: A unique name, it has a Teutonic origin and translates to a fierce and brave warrior.

- Benat: The German name is given to those who are as brave as a bear.

- Benin: Not only is the name short, it is quite poetic as well. It has a Latin origin, and means the loved one.

- Bevan: The Celtic name means a brave and courageous soldier.

- Bharat: The Hindi name is certainly quite unique. It means the one likes to support a thoughtful cause.

- Blair: A name that should definitely be loved by all the nature enthusiasts. It means the child of the fields. The timeless English name will certainly be loved by all.

- Bran: Short and meaningful, Bran comes from both Celtic and Welsh origin and translates to a raven.

- Caleb: The Biblical name will certainly be a hit amongst your friends and family. It will inspire your boy to strive for excellence as well.

- Chad: The name has both Celtic as well as English origin. Though, it translates to a warrior in both the cases. Chad is both, a short and a poignant name for a baby boy.

- Cyrus: Now, Cyrus is certainly a royal name. Also, it has a certain modern edge to it that makes it so timeless. The name has a Persian origin and translates to "the sun". The name is linked to the legendary emperor of Persia.

- Clive: Once a popular choice, the name is gradually becoming a favorite. The English name means the one who lives nearby a cliff.

- Cohen: The Hebrew originated name has a religious meaning to it. It means priest or a noble person. It is also widely used as a surname.

- Clyde: The Scottish name has a regional meaning, but it has become a globally accepted name. It has been originated from the river Clide (Clyde) in Scotland.

- Conan: The name has been used by plenty of celebrities as well. A common name in Ireland, it is still not that popular in other parts of the world. It means someone who is intelligent.

- Cortez: The Spanish name was once widely used as a last name. It means the one who is courteous to others.

- Caillen: The Gaelic name is perfect for those parents who have been waiting for their little one for a long time. It means an awaited or precious child.

- Cal: The one who is bold and fearless.

- Calais: Not only the name is quite poetic, but it has such a deep meaning as well. The Latin name translates to the son of the north wind.

- Carling: It means little champion in Gaelic.

- Casimir: Go international with this poignant name that has a Polish origin. It literally translates to the announcement or commencement of peace and will certainly make your little one stand out from the crowd.

- Caspian: There are lots of Irish folktales associated with the word Caspian. It means the one who came from the sea.

- Chayton: The Native American name will be a hit among the town. It means falcon and has a peculiar ring to it.

- Cian: Also spelled as "Chinan", it has a Gaelic-Irish origin and translates to the one who has an ancient soul.

- Conall: The Celtic name means the one who is a strong opponent in a battle or a fierce warrior. On the other hand, the Irish translation of it is the one who is highly and superior.

- Cyril: The Greek name was originally given to the Saint Cyril. It also has a timeless and modern ring to it.

- Dean: The English name is given to those who belong to a valley. It would be adored by all the nature lovers.

- Dexter: It means the one who is always right. It is originated from Latin.

- Drew: It was once a popular name in the South and is again gaining immense popularity. It means someone who is brave and honest. It is also preferred as a shorter version for "Andrew".

- Duncan: The royal name was originally given to the Gaelic Emperor Duncan.

- Darren: The English name means someone who is born to achieve greatness.

- Darryl: The English name actually came from the French surname D'Arel.

- Dmitri: The Greek-Russian origin name is now accepted globally as a cool yet timeless choice that is loved by young boys for its royal touch. It can be spelled as "Demetri" or "Demitri".

- Damek: Damek has been originated from Czech and means the son of the earth.

- Dann: Short yet impactful, Dann has a Hebrew origin and means someone who judges things in a positive manner.

- Deron: The Armenian name has a timeless charm. It means the one who belongs to the God.

- Errol: It has both German as well as Latin origin and translates to a wise or noble man.

- Eagan: The beautiful Irish name means someone who is fierce and bold.

- Edan: An effortless and natural name, it has a Celtic origin and means fire.

- Edwald: The name might sound similar to "Edward" but it has a different meaning. The English name means someone who is wealthy and prosperous.

- Eero: Also known as a popular alternative to "Eric", it is a Finnish name. It literally translates to an eternal ruler.

- Egan: This Irish name translates to someone who is brave and wise.

- Ekon: The Nigerian name means someone who is strong and brave.

- Elazar: The biblical name translates to the helper of the god.

- Emery: A popular alternative to "Amery", it means someone who is powerful and brave.

- Emiyn: The name is certainly a unique one and sounds poetic. It has a Welsh origin and means waterfall.

- Ethen: This Latin name means someone who has a strong well-being.

- Emrys: The royal name will certainly take your little one to places. It has a Gaelic origin and means the one who can't be destroyed.

- Enar: The Norse-originated name will be your favorite as well. It means fighter or warrior.

- Eren: The Turkish name translates to "Saint".

- Everard: The English name was once a famous title. It means someone who is brave and kind-hearted.

- Evin: The Irish name means the one who is swift and flawless.

- Ewan: The Scottish name translates to youthfulness. If you know your boy will stay forever-young and would be a free spirit, then you should definitely go ahead with this one.

- Flynn: The literal translation of this Irish name is "the son of a red-haired man". If you think your boy suits this description, then you should definitely go ahead with it.

- Fredrik: The Swedish name is gaining immense popularity these days. It means a peaceful emperor or king.

- Faris: It has multiple meanings and origins. The English translation of it is the one who is strong as iron. In Arabic, it means a knight or a brave horse-rider.

- Fadil: The Arabic name means someone who is superior and intelligent.

- Faine: Doesn't Faine have a peculiar ring to it? In English, it means someone who is humble and well brought up.

- Faraz: The Persian name means someone who is superior of all and always leads the way.

- Farren: The Irish name has a thoughtful meaning. It translates to the one who love adventures. There are plenty of different spelling variations of it.

- Fay: It means raven in Irish.

- Felicien: Now that's a unique name. Not only it sounds great, it also has a thoughtful meaning. The French name means someone who stays happy and content. It is spelled as Felician in Latin.

- Fenris: The Norse originated name was used to depict a mystical wolf.

- Galvin: The name became widely popular after being opted by famous musicians. It takes us back to the Victorian era as it has a timeless charm. The English name means white hawk.

- Grant: Also spelled as "Grantt", it has a French origin. Though, it is also a common word in English these days. It means to bestow or provide.

- Gideon: A futuristic name, it is something that is both timeless and classy. It has a Hebrew origin and means the one who wins against evil spirits.

- Grayson: The English name usually translates to the one who is the son of a gray-haired man. It is a common surname, which has gained immense popularity after the John Green book.

- Glen: It has a Gaelic origin and is used to depict someone who belongs to a valley.

- Gerard: The German name has gained immense popularity the world over. It depicts a brave warrior.

- Garner: The name has a peculiar French origin. It was originally used a common surname, but has come out as a first name option these days. It translates to someone who is the keeper of the grain.

- Gil: The Hebrew name translates to contentment and happiness.

- Gustav: The Scandinavian name is given to emperors and eminent rulers.

- Gunther: The name has been originated from the heart of Germany and means a brave warrior or knight.

- Gace: The name certainly has a crisp and a poetic ring to it. It means to pledge or promise in French.

- Galen: A Gaelic name that has a meaning as serene as its sound. It means something serene and calm. It is also spelled as "Galyn".

- Ganesh: A Hindu name, which is given to one of the ancient gods (son of Shiva). Ganesh is also widely known as the God of good times and prosperity.

- Garrick: The simple yet unique English name is given to a ruler and a spear-warrior.

- Gelasius: There can't be a better decision than naming your little boy after the respected Pope. The name has a Greek origin and literally translates to "laughter".

- Gennadi: This unique name has been originated from Russian and translates to someone who is kind and generous.

- Godwine: The name certainly has a meaning as good as its sound. The English name translates to God's friend. Simply put an extra "o" to make it Goodwine and the meaning to be changed to a good friend.

- Gregos: The name means the one who is vigilant in nature. It has a Greek origin.

- Helmer: The Native American name is both rugged and timeless. It means someone who can fight the fury and anger. It also means the one who is quite deterministic to achieve greatness.

- Hugh: The name has a poetic pronunciation. It has both German and English origin and means someone who is kind and intelligent.

- Harvey: This name has not lost its charm. It has a rugged appeal that would age well with your boy. It has been derived from French and means the one who is not afraid to go to a battle (a fierce warrior).

- Hubert: This German word means someone who has a bright spirit. Saint Hubert made it a household name.

- Hartley: All that nature-lovers would love this name. The English name represents someone who belongs to the meadows.

- Helmut: It has a futuristic ring to it with a thoughtful meaning. The name has a German origin and symbolizes bravery.

- Horus: It is one such royal name that will certainly get your little boy noticed. The Egyptian name was originally given to the Lord of the sky.

- Hael: It goes well with the famous name "Gael", but it has a different meaning. The Welsh origin name means the one who is healthy and has a good spirit.

- Hafez: This Persian name means the one who protect others.

- Isaac: The English name has a biblical origin, as the name was given to the son of Abraham and Sarah.

- Imanol: The Hebrew name has a poetic touch to it. It means "God is with us", which certainly signifies how thoughtful this name is.

- Inteus: The Native American word was originally used to depict those who are brave and not ashamed of anything.

It would definitely make a remarkable name for your boy.

- Joel: The biblical name has a Hebrew-Latin original and is quite a popular choice these days.

- Jarrod: A rugged and sporty name, it would definitely age well with your boy. The English name is given to those who are strong and healthy.

- Jaffan: It is such a unique name that would be loved by all. The African origin name would be definitely picked by nature-lovers. It means a stream or a flowing river.

- Jair: The biblical name is not commonly used by parents these days. It has a Hebrew origin and translates to "the one who shines bright".

- Jairo: The sound of it is something that sets it apart from every other name. It is pronounced as "hi-row" and has been originated from Spanish. It means the same as Jair – the one who shines.

- Keith: It is one such name that can never go out of the trends. It has an Irish origin and literally translates to forest or dense woods.

- Kieran: The Gaelic origin name was given to those babies who have dark and shiny hair. You can definitely use it and let your little boy own it with time.

- Keanue: This beautiful Hawaiian name has a meaning as light as it sounds. It translates to the cool breeze over a mountain.

- Kamal: The name has different meanings. In Hindi, it means lotus while in Arabic it signifies perfection or flawlessness. Needless to say, it will give your boy that peculiar exotic charm.

- Kaelan: Often spelled as "Caelan" as well, this Gaelic name means the one who is white and fair.

- Keane: The Irish name has recently gained immense popularity after the successful band. It was originally used as a last name and means ancient or something which is old and authentic.

- Landon: This English name has a typical Victorian charm to it. It will add a perfect royal touch to your boy's character. It means someone who came from the hills.

- Louis: Originally, a name for boys, it is rapidly coming into unisex territory. It has been taken from French and means a warrior.

- Lamar: Another French signature name, it means the one who belongs to the sea or ocean.

- Leif: This is one of the most unique and meaningful names for a boy. The Scandinavian name means someone who is a descendant. Its literal translation is "son" and would age perfectly with your boy.

- Ludwig: Be inspired from the Bavarian emperor and name your son after one of the greatest German fighters.

- Leander: The name certainly has a perfect ring. It has been originated from German and means lion or lion-like.

- Lamarr: A common last name, it has been originated from French and means someone who belongs to the sea.

- Lazarus: The Hebrew name has a strong biblical reference and means helper of God.

- Luka: The Russian version of Lucas, it translates to light.

- Lennox: Originally a boy name that has been originated from the Shakespeare's play, The Macbeth. Though, it has come out as a prominent unisex name.

- Lev: Crisp and meaningful, it has been originated from Hebrew and means lion.

- Lachlan: The Scottish name means "a land of lakes". It would definitely be adored by any nature lover.

- Laius: The Greek origin name was given to the father of Oedipus.

- Lambert: Also a common last name, it has been originated from German and means a land of bright lights.

- Leonel: The name has recently gained immense popularity. It has been originated from Spanish and means a young lion.

- Leroux: A common surname in France, it is often used as a first name as well. It translates to "the red-haired one".

- Loxias: This Greek name certainly has a thoughtful meaning. It was one of the titles given to Apollo and translates to a male oracle.

- Micah: Show some love for your little one by choosing this biblical name for him that was once given to a prophet.

- Miguel: This Spanish name translates to the one who is similar to a lord or a king.

- Milo: Milo has two contrasting meanings. While in English it means protected, the Greek translation of it is "a destroyer".

- Manuel: This well-spirited Spanish name translates to the phrase "God is with us", which is commonly used in Spain.

- Mateo: A common name in Latin America, it has a Spanish origin and translates to "a gift given by the Gods".

- Murphy: The Irish name is certainly an everlasting one. It means sea warrior.

- Magnus: Give your little boy a futuristic name by choosing Magnus. It has multiple meanings. The Danish translation of it is "excellent" or "great". It has been used as a prominent title to glorify Scandinavian kings.

- Melvin: The name has a Celtic origin and translates to a good friend. It also means leader.

- Matthias: A unique name, it has been originated from German and has a strong biblical associated with it. The name has come out as a common alternative to "Mathew" and means "god's gift".

- Marcelo: Marcelo is definitely one of the most masculine names of all. It has an Italian origin and is given to someone who is as strong as a hammer.

- Makoto: If you want to go international, then this Japanese name will surely be a keeper. It means truth or reality.

- Macauley: This timeless Scottish name means righteousness.

- Mikel: A variation to "Michael", it has Hebrew roots and means god's gift.

- Mika: Derived from "Mikel", the Hebrew name has the same meaning of a "god's gift".

- Maverick: This stylish American name gained popularity after the famous movie. It means independent or something that can't be tamed.

- Maged: This Egyptian name is given to someone who is glorious and magnificent.

- Mahpee: This Native American name translates to "sky" and sounds pretty adorable too.

- Maher: The name is quite famous in the Middle East and is gradually finding its way to other parts of the word. It has an Arabic origin and means skillful. Though, there is also an Irish version of the same name, which translates to kind and generous.

- Malyn: This English name translates to a young warrior.

- Manfrit: Manfrit has a German origin and means someone who spreads peace and serenity. Needless to say, its meaning would be loved by all.

- Manu: Short yet thoughtful, this Hindu-origin name is linked with mythology. The literal translation of Manu is "ruler of the world". Manu was also the first man to walk on earth (like Adam).

- Manzo: If you are having a third son, then this Japanese name would be a perfect choice. It translates to "the third-born son who is strong and kind".

- Marlowe: This English name has a peculiar poetic touch to it. It means someone who came from the mountains or the lakes.

- Massimo: A futuristic name, it has been originated from Latin and means "the greatest".

- Matvey: This Russian name means a gift given by the god.

- Maynor: Maynor has both German as well as French origin and means powerful and strong.

- Mayne: The French name translates to a powerful and driven boy.

- Meinke: It has been originated from German and means something which is firm and impactful.

- Meir: It certainly has a perfect sound to it. Originated from Hebrew, it means the one who is enlightened.

- Melchior: It has a Persian origin and a strong biblical connection. Melchior was one of the three wise kings who traveled with Jesus. Who wouldn't like to name their baby after one of the wise kings?

- Mercer: It means Merchant in English.

- Merlyn: The mystical name is gradually making its way in the ongoing trends. It has a Celtic origin and means "from the sea". According to Irish folk tales, Merlyn (also spelled as "Merlin" at times) was a magician and King Arthur's advisor.

- Mervyn: This stylish name has a French origin and means "a wise friend".

- Milos: Milos has an attractive sound. It has been originated from Czech and means someone who is pleasant and kind.

- Mingan: This Native American word is used to depict a gray wolf.

- Mohsen: It has a Persian origin and means someone who does kind acts.

- Montez: This Italian name literally translates to "mountain".

- Morpheus: If you are a fan of Greek mythology, you are going to love this name. It means the one who brings pleasant dreams.

- Morrissey: This Irish name is quite popular in the local regions and is reaching to other parts of the world as well. It means "from the sea".

- Noel: A popular choice among Christmas-lovers, it has a French origin and quite literally translates to "Christmas".

- Noah: Another biblical name, it has gained immense popularity amongst parents. It has a Hebrew origin and means "to confront someone".

- Nathan: It is one such name that can never go out of the style. The Hebrew originated name means a gift from the god.

- Nolan: Also used as a surname, it has a Celtic and Irish origin and means a wise and noble man.

- Nicholas: The Greek originated name is associated with many nicknames like Nick or Nico. It means victorious.

- Neil: This Gaelic originated name means a champion or victorious warrior.

- Nigel: This English-Celtic name translates to "victorious".

- Norman: A famous English name, it means someone who came from the north.

- Noland: It means noble in Celtic.

- Nevan: Short and meaningful, it means holy and pious in Irish.

- Natal: If your boy is born at Christmas, then you can't think of a better name than this. It has been originated from Spanish and literally translates to "born at Christmas".

- Nadav: it has a Hebrew origin and translates to noble.

- Naaman: It means pleasant and kind in Hebrew.

- Naiser: This thoughtful name came from a local African language and means founder or creator.

- Narius: It means "the one who stays cheerful" in Latin.

- Norvin: The Celtic name means "a friend who came from the north".

- Owen: This likable name has a Celtic origin and means a young warrior.

- Orlando: This beautiful name came into the limelight after the Shakespeare's play. It has a Spanish origin and means someone who is renowned and famous.

- Otis: A German originated name, it means the one who is wealthy.

- Odin: A Norse origin name, Odin was the god of war, poetry, and culture.

- Oriel: It means eagle in Russian.

- Owsin: An English name, it means "god's friend".

- Odion: If you have given birth to twins, then you should definitely pick this one. This Egyptian name translates to "the first-born child of the twins".

- Orion: This Greek name will certainly make a unique and thoughtful choice. Orion is the name of the famous constellation. He was the hunter-god and son of Poseidon who emerged from the fire.

- Phoenix: Give your boy this inspiring name. It translates to "deep red" and is related to the legendary bird.

- Prescott: The English name translates to a priest's cottage and is used as a common surname as well.

- Payden: It means "from a fighter's den". This English name is also used as a last name quite often.

- Quinton: Also used as a common surname, the French translation of it is "the fifth". In English, it means Queen's farm.

- Reuben: A Hebrew originated name that has a biblical connection. Reuben was the son of Jacob and Leah.

- Reid: This English name means a red-head individual and can be spelled as "Reed" as well.

- Reece: It means passionate and enthusiastic in Welsh.

- Randolph: This English name translates to a "shielded wolf".

- Roderick: Name your child after the famous European ruler. It certainly has a perfect royal touch to it.

- Rupert: It has a German origin and means someone who is bright and famous.

- Remus: An ancient Latin name that has not lost its charm. Remus was one of the founders of Rome.

- Raydon: It has a strong French and English association with it and translates to a counselor or a wise man.

- Rafael: Also spelled as "Raphael" at times, it was made famous by the renowned sportsman. It has been originated from Spanish and means "version of".

- Rafi: It means someone who is content and kind in Arabic.

- Raidon: This Japanese name will surely make your little one stand out. It is the name of the Japanese thunder god.

- Raj: It means emperor in Hindi.

- Rama: Derived from Sanskrit, it means god-like.

- Raynor: The Norse originated name was given to the warrior or lord of judgment.

- Rei: This Japanese name means "to strive for perfection".

- Reiner: It has a German origin and translates to "counsel".

- Rene: In French, it means "to rise again" or "reborn". The Spanish name "Renato" has the same meaning and can be a great choice for your boy's name.

- Renzo: If you are having a third-born son, then this is just the perfect choice. It has a Japanese origin and means "the third son".

- Rhys: It means the one who is passionate or enthusiastic. It has a Welsh origin.

- Rondel: In French, a short poem of 14 lines is called a Rondel. It would make a meaningful and poetic name for sure.

- Royd: This Scandinavian word means "the one who dwells in the forest".

- Spencer: It means "keeper" or "protector".

- Sean: The Irish name means "God is kind".

- Shane: A popular variant of Sean.

- Shea: A majestic Irish name which translates to "hawk" or "hawk-like". "Shay" is a popular alternative to it.

- Sebastian: The Latin originates name means "reverend" and has a poetic and masculine ring to it.

- Skeet: A futuristic name, it means "swift" in English.

- Shaw: A common Irish name, it means someone who came from the shades.

- Shiloh: A Hebrew name, it translates to the one who favors peace.

- Silos: In Latin, it means the one who came from the forest.

- Sven: In Swedish, it means "youth".

- Sewell: A Teutonic name, it means "mighty at sea".

- Stefon: A popular alternative to "Stephan", it means "crown".

- Sabir: It has an Arabic origin and means the one who is patient and kind.

- Sagar: It means someone who is wise in English. In Hindi, it translates to "ocean".

- Sandor: It is a thoughtful Hungarian name, which means defender of mankind.

- Santo: A widely known Italian name, it means something pious or holy.

- Sasha: The Russian name means defender of the mankind.

- Seb: Seb is known as the Egyptian god of earth.

- Selik: It has been originated from German and translates to "blessed", which makes it such a thoughtful name.

- Shaan: It means "peaceful" in Hebrew and "pride" in Hindi.

- Sigmund: The German name means "victorious protector". Its other variant "Sigurd" means the same in Norse.

- Silvio: In Latin, it means the one who came from the forest.

- Stetson: Its literal translation is "cowboy hat", which makes it a great country name.

- Strom: It means "tree" in Czech.

- Svens: IT has a Swedish origin and translates to the one who is youthful.

- Tyson: It means ruler of the thunder in English.

- Theo: The Greek originated name translates to "given by the gods". It is gaining immense popularity these days.

- Tyrell: Translates to a warrior, it has a Norse origin.

- Troy: It means "growing" in Norse.

- Tyrus: A masculine name, it translates to "thunder" in English.

- Terrel: It means powerful and strong in both German and English.

- Tahbert: The name has a German origin and translates to "to praise someone".

- Talus: A Greek mythology name, Talus was the son of Perdix.

- Taren: It means "thunder" in Welsh. It can also be spelled as "Tarran".

- Taurus: If he shares the same zodiac sign, then there is no harm in naming him "Taurus". The Latin originated name is quite masculine and translates to "bull".

- Tavin: It means "one of the twins". If you are having twins, then Tavin should definitely be shortlisted by you. In Scottish, "Tavish" has the same meaning and can be opted as a second name as well. After all, who wouldn't love to name their twins "Tavin" and "Tavish"

- Teague: It has a Gaelic influence to it and means "a poet".

- Thacker: It means "twin" in Irish.

- Theseus: Every literature lover would adore this name. Shakespeare made it famous from his play "A Midsummer's Night Dream".

- Thor: The god of thunder.

- Tobyn: This Green originated name translates to the phrase "God is good".

- Torin: The Norse originated title, given to Thor's fighter.

- Urien: This Hebrew originated name translates to "light".
- Ulric: It has a favorable ring to it. This German originated name means someone who has a strong determination and will.
- Vaughn: Also spelled as "Vaughin" at times, it has a Russia origin and is associated with something royal.
- Vaughan: It has been originated from Hindi and means "King of serpents".
- Vadim: A beautiful Hebrew name, it translates to the phrase "in God, we find strength".
- Vinn: The Italian version of Victor.
- Valentino: Poetic and masculine, this Latin originated name means strong and brave. It was also the name of the famous Saint Valentino.
- Valen: The Swedish name translates to someone who is powerful and fierce.
- Vidor: It has a Hebrew origin and means someone who is adored by others.
- Varun: It means "wind" in Hindi and "beloved" in Irish.
- Vishnu: The supreme Indian god.
- Wayne: Used as a Scandinavian surname, it is now a favorable choice of a name all over the world.
- Wyatt: It means the one who protects the world.
- Waller: It means a peaceful ruler in German.
- Warrick: The Latin originated word means "truthful" or simply "true".

- Wartun: In English, it means the one who lives in the meadows.

- Xenos: It means "bright" in Arabic. It also has a Spanish association and means "owner of a house".

- Ximen: In Greek, it means "ruler of the heroes", which makes it quite legendary.

- Yavin: Originated from Arabic, it means simple and easy.

- Yves: It has a Russian and French origin to it and is associated with nature. It means "from the woods" and is pronounced as "eev".

- Zain: It has been originated from Swahili and translates to "flower".

- Zahir: A name with different meanings. In Arabic, it means "something which is known to all" while in Armenian, it means "flower".

- Zev: Translates to "an older twin", it has been originated from Africa.

- Ziv: In Teutonic, it means "free" and "liberated".

- Zvi: Short and impactful, it means "good" in Swahili.

We are sure you would be able to pick some or other kind of thoughtful name for your little boy from our list. To make things easier for you, we provided a wide range of names with their respective origin and meaning. This would help you handpick some of the most unique names for your little one.

If you are not sure about the gender of your unborn child or are expecting a baby girl, then move to our next chapter. We have come up with a comprehensive collection of names for girls as well in our next chapter that would be of great help to you. Read on and pick just the perfect name for your little girl.

Chapter 7 – Unique and Meaningful Names For Girls

Too often, finding just the right kind of name for your little girl can be a tedious task. There can be so many options out there and handpick a few of the best choices can take a lot of time. Don't worry! We are here to help you so that you can give your child a remarkable name.

We have shortlisted some of the most meaningful and unique names for girls. Simply go through our thoughtfully drafted list and pick a perfect one for your angel!

- Amelia: A romantic and poetic name, it means someone who is perseverant. It has been originated from Latin.

- Adele: Made famous by the renowned British artist, it was originally given to Saint Adele. It has a German original and means "a kind wolf".

- Alicia: The Spanish name is translated to "noble" and is considered as an alternative to "Alice".

- Adriana: This dreamy name was first adopted in Shakespeare's play "Comedy of Errors".

- Aileen: It has an Irish origin and means "light".

- Autumn: It can be given to your girl if she is born in the fall.

- Aida: This English name is quite poetic and lovable. It means "wealthy" in English.

- Abequa: This Native American name literally translates to the one who is homely or likes to stay at home.

- Abir: This short and meaningful name has an Arabic origin and translates to "a desirable fragrance".

- Adana: Give your daddy's girl this Nigerian name, which means "her father's daughter".

- Adira: The Arabic name translates to "strong" and "determined".

- Aerwyna: This English name certainly has a ring to it and means the one who is a friend of the sea.

- Agata: A Greek originated name, which means "kind hearted".

- Agna: It means "the one who is pure" in Greek. The Danish version of the name is "Agneta" which can also be a great choice for your girl's name.

- Ahana: An Irish name, which means "someone who came from the forts".

- Aife: Be inspired from this Celtic name which is given to female warriors.

- Airlia: This thoughtful name means "eternal" in Greek.

- Aislin: The Irish name is a title and is given to those who have a vision.

- Aldis: Show your love for a southern romance with this poetic name. It means "from the old house" in English.

- Alethea: The Greek Goddess of truth. In Greek, it translates to "truth".

- Athena: Step it up by naming your little one after the Greek goddess of wisdom. The city of Athens is named after her as well.

- Aleta: Give your little angel this Danish name, which means "the little winged one".

- Alexus: A post-modern name, it means "defender of the humanity".

- Alita: It means "winged" in English and "noble" in Spanish.

- Aliza: It means "joy" in Hebrew.

- Allis: This Teutonic name means "noble".

- Altair: The name has an Arabic origin and translates to "bird".

- Alva: It means "white" in German. It is used as a symbol for pure and divine.

- Ama: This short yet poetic name has different meanings. It translates to "eagle" in Norse, while it is given to those who are born on a Saturday in Africa.

- Amaranda: It means "unfading flower" in Greek. It became "Amarante" in French.

- Amare: In African, it means the one who is strong and wise. It can also be spelled as "Amari".

- Amaya: This Japanese name means "midnight rain" and is often used in Japanese poetry.

- Ambre: This French word is used to depict the color Amber.

- Ambrosia: It means "immortal" in Greek.

- Amia: It means "beloved" in English. It can also be spelled as "Amie".

- Amor: A name that would definitely be loved by all. It means "love" in Spanish.

- Analena: It means the one who is graceful. It has a Spanish origin.

- Analise: This Hebrew originated name means "graced by the god".

- Anat: In Hebrew, it means "to sing a song". The name certainly has a peculiar ring to it.

- Anjali: It means "god's messenger" in Hindi.

- Anora: This unique name means "light" in English.

- Anthia: This Greek name translates to "lady of flowers".

- Apsara: The name is associated with Hindu mythology and is usually given to exotic nymphs.

- Aria: It Latin, it means "air" or "melody".

- Assana: It means "waterfall" in Irish.

- Aurora: The poetic name was originally given to the Sleeping Beauty.

- Austen: Be inspired from the Egyptian mythology. Austen was one of the most powerful Egyptian female gods.

- Avis: It means "bird" in Latin.

- Ayala: It has a Hebrew origin and means "gazelle".

- Beth: The unisex name is now widely used for girls. It is both contemporary and thoughtful. It means "home" in Hebrew.

- Blair: This beautiful name means the one who came from the fertile lands. It has a Celtic origin.

- Brenna: The name has a Celtic origin and is ideally translated to "raven".

- Blossom: This is one such name that would be adored by all the nature lovers. It is associated with flower and spring.

- Bella: The name became a popular choice after the famous Twilight series. It has a Latin origin and means "fair" or "beautiful".

- Becca: Becca is one of the most everlasting and timeless names of all. It means someone who is extremely captivating and beautiful.

- Brylee: This Native American name translates to "noble" or "meadow". It is both, fresh and thoughtful.

- Baha: This Persian name has its own charm. It means something valuable and irreplaceable.

- Basia: In Polish, Basia means someone who is exotic or belongs to a foreign land.

- Beda: In English, Beda means a female warrior.

- Bellona: The Latin word was originally given to the goddess of war.

- Berdine: It means glamorous or gorgeous in German.

- Biana: The Latin word translates to "fair".

- Brooklyn: One of the trendiest names for girls, it means someone who likes to live nearby a brook. The NYC borough made it quite famous all over the world.

- Claire: The French name translates to someone who is bright and clear.

- Cassandra: The Greek originated name means "helper of god".

- Christine: Go a little international and give your daughter this French name, which is a European take on "Christina".

- Cora: Originated from Greek, it symbolizes someone who came from the sea.

- Colleen: It means "girl" in Irish.
- Celina: Originates from Greek, it depicts the "goddess of the moon".
- Chandra: This Sanskrit name translates to "the moon".
- Chiara: It means someone who is bright or full of light.
- Cadyna: This unique name will certainly make your daughter stand out. It means "melody" or "rhythmic" in English.
- Calandra: It means "beautiful" and has been taken from Greek.
- Calliope: Taken from Greek, it means someone who has a beautiful voice.
- Caralisa: In Latin, it means "beloved".
- Carina: The name certainly has a ring to it. Carina is one of the brightest stars in Orion (the constellation).
- Catia: The name has a distinctive pronunciation and means "pure" in Greek.
- Chaya: Short yet meaningful, it means "life" in Hebrew, which makes it one of the most thoughtful names out there.
- Clea: A smart and smart name, usually termed as an abbreviation to "Cleopatra".
- Cosette: It has been derived from French and means someone who is victorious.
- Cyra: Originated from Persian, it is the feminine form of "Cyrus" and means "the sun".
- Delilah: The name is originated from Hebrew and means "desired". It certainly has a timeless charm to it.

- Dakota: This Native American name is quite a charmer. It is used to represent allies or friends.

- Darlene: Derived from Old English, it means "Darling".

- Danica: The name has been originated from Slavic and literally translates to "a moving star".

- Davina: It means "cherished" or "beloved" in Hebrew.

- Dael: It has been derived from Dutch and translates to a "small valley".

- Deane: It means "divine" and would go well as a middle name as well.

- Dessa: Originated from Greek, it symbolizes the one who likes to wander.

- Devika: It has been originated from Sanskrit and means "little goddess".

- Devona: it has been derived from Celtic and means "the divine one".

- Domina: This sophisticated name has been derived from Latin and means "lady".

- Drew: A unisex name, it would be surely be embraced by your daughter. It is one of those names that would age really well with time. It means "brave" in English.

- Ella: Ella is one such name that would be loved by all. There is just something about "Ella" which makes it so poetic. It has been originated from German and means "the one who is complete".

- Evelyn: This meaningful name would age really well with your daughter. It means "wished for" in English and "life" in Celtic.

- Erica: The Norse originated name translates to "eternal ruler".

- Elena: It means "light" in Greek.

- Elaine: The French version of Elena, it also means "light".

- Elsa: Made popular by the Disney movie, it means "pledged to the god" in English. It has been originated from German.

- Elsie: The German name means "noble".

- Ethel: It means "kind" or "noble" in English.

- Essie: Originated from Latin, it means "star". The Finnish version of it is "Essi".

- Evonne: A name with a unique pronunciation, it is the female derivate of "Yves".

- Earie: This Scottish name is not that common in the world. It translates to "the one who came from the east".

- Eberta: A Teutonic name, it means "intelligent".

- Eda: Short yet meaningful, it means "wealthy" in English. It can also be referred as "Edina".

- Edwinna: This English name translates to someone who can be friends with others easily.

- Eeva: It means "life" in Hebrew and can also be spelled as "Eva".

- Elanna: A Hebrew originated work, it means "oak tree". It can also be written as "Elaine".

- Eleanore: Give your daughter a unique name by keeping "Eleanore" in your shortlist. It has been originated from Greek and means "light". It can also be written as "Eleanora".

- Electra: If you know your daughter is going to be bright like the sun then there is no harm is giving her this Greek name, which means "a fiery sun".

- Elene: It means "light" in Greek.

- Elin: The Swedish alternative to "Elena", it also means "light".

- Elita: The name has different meanings. It means "the chosen one" in Latin and "the one who is winged" in English.

- Ellery: Commonly used as a last name, it means "happiness" or "joyful" in English.

- Ellinor: There is just something about this Swedish name that makes it so attractive. It has been derived from Eleanore.

- Elora: A modern name, it is linked with positivity and light.

- Elva: Derived from the word "Elfin", it has an Irish origin and means "counselor".

- Elyta: In English, it means "winged".

- Emira: The Latin word means "someone who should be praised".

- Enrika: It means "ruler" and has been derived from Teutonic.

- Eris: Consider naming your daughter after the Greek goddess.

- Erline: If you are from Ireland, then consider naming your daughter "Erline". It means "a girl from Ireland".

- Eshe: An African originated name, it means "life".

- Esta: Derived from Latin, it literally translates to "east".

- Evia: It means "the one who lives" in both Latin and Hebrew.

- Faith: The name has a peculiar southern charm which makes it such a hit. We all know the positive meaning of this English name. If your daughter has more siblings or twins, you can always give them relevant names like "Hope" or "Grace".

- Fiona: This poetic name will certainly encourage your little girl to go in arts. It translates to "fair" in Latin.

- Frances: If you have French roots, then you can carry on your heritage by naming your girl this patriotic name, which means "the one who is from France". It also translates to "free form" in Latin.

- Flavia: A name given to one of the Roman legends, it means "golden" in Latin.

- Freda: An attractive alternative to "Frieda", it translates to a "peaceful ruler" in Greek.

- Fanya: This beautiful name means "free" in Slavic.

- Fern: It will be a hit among all the nature-lovers, as it literally means "fauna" or "little plants".

- Fairen: This Native American name translates to "beautiful".

- Fani: Short yet meaningful, it means "free" in Latin.

- Farida: An Arabic name, it means "unique" or "priceless".

- Farin: It means "adventurous" in English.

- Faustine: Definitely a unique one, it means "the one who is fortunate". It has a Latin origin.

- Filia: A thoughtful Greek name, it literally translates to "daughter".

- Flede: A Teutonic name, it means "swift".

- Grace: A classic English name, it would be loved by all your friends and family.

- Giselle: One of those timeless names, it has a French origin and means "pledge".

- Gloria: It would definitely age well with your little one. It has been derived from Latin and means "glory". The simplicity of this one makes it such a hit.

- Gina: It can be used as a nickname for your little one. It means "well-born" in Greek.

- Gretchen: This German name has a meaning as attractive as its pronunciation. It means "little pearl".

- Gladys: It has been derived from Welsh and translates to someone who is fair and beautiful.

- Gillian: One of those futuristic names that will certainly make your daughter stand out, it means "youthful" and has been derived from Latin.

- Gretel: It means "pearl" in German.

- Gweneth: There is just something about Gweneth, which makes it so irresistible. It means "blessed" in Celtic. It can also be spelled as "Gwynth" or "Gwenith".

- Gael: Short yet sweet, it translates to "joyful". Originally a unisex name, it is now commonly used as a girl's name. It can also be spelled as "Gale".

- Galatia: It is associated with the Greek mythological tale of Pygmalion, who fell in love with Galatia (the ivory sculpture). She was brought to life by Aphrodite. It translates to "the white one" and sounds as exotic as its name.

- Gavina: A Scottish name, it means "white hawk".

- Giana: The Latin word which literally translates to "God is gracious".

- Gila: A Hebrew name, it means "eternal happiness".

- Golnaz: A Persian name, it is also commonly spelled as "Gulnaz", which translates to "as beautiful as a flower".

- Hayley: Give your little one this fun and cute name, which means "from the hay meadows" in English.

- Hermione: A treat for all the Harry Potter fans, give your daughter this legendary name if you are also a fan of the series. It is a French name and means "harmony".

- Helia: It means "sun" in Greek.

- Halia: One of the most thoughtful Hawaiian names of all, it translates to the phrase "with you, we remember a loved one".

- Hadeya: The Arabic name translates to "gift".

- Hasna: It means "beautiful" and "feminine" in Arabic and "to laugh" in Hindi.

- Haya: This short yet thoughtful Hebrew name means "to live".

- Hesper: This Greek name translates to "evening star" in English.

- Ivy: A treat to all the nature-lovers, it is the name given to one of the most beautiful flowers in the world.

- Irene: The Greek work translates to "peace".

- Isla: A name given to a Scottish coast, it is gradually making its way to other parts of the world as well.

- India: If you have a love for the country, then there is no harm is naming your daughter after one of the oldest civilizations. It is a Sanskrit name and translates to "river".

- Iliana: A beautiful choice, it has been originated from Greek and means "light".

- Irma: The German name stands for "strength" and "courage".

- Ivana: The Czech phrase stands for "God has been kind and gracious".

- Ivory: The name of the color, it is usually associated with "white" and "fair".

- Iola: The Greek version of the color "violet".

- Inis: It means "an island" in Irish.

- Imani: The name translates to "faith" in African.

- Indigo: A variant of the color blue.

- Indrani: An Indian name, it is the name of one of the many female goddesses.

- Joanna: A French name, which translates to "gift from the god".

- June: Originally the name was given to a Roman god. If your girl is born during the month of June, then it can be a great choice for her name as well.

- Jolene: It means "beautiful" and has a French origin.

- Jeanne: It means "a gift from the god" and is a common alternative to "Jean" or "Jane".

- Joslyn: A medieval middle name, it is now a popular choice for a girl's name.

- Janaya: This English name literally translates to "God has all the answers".

- Jayanti: It means "victory" in Hindi.

- Justina: The feminine version of "Justin", it means "fair" in Latin.

- Kya: This futuristic name means "light" and is a popular alternative to "Cyra".

- Kaila: If you know you have given birth to a diva, then why not give her this chic and hip Hawaiian name, which means "style".

- Kailani: Another Hawaiian name, it translates to "sky".

- Kaia: It translates to "originated from the earth" and has Greek roots.

- Kaira: A Scandinavian name, it translates to "pure".

- Kala: It means "princess" in Hawaiian.

- Kali: An African originated name, it means "energetic". It is also a name given to one of the most powerful Hindu goddesses.

- Kalyca: It means "rosebud" in Greek.

- Kami: This original Japanese name translates to "pure aura" and has a peculiar ring to it.

- Kani: Originated from Hawaiian, it means "sound".

- Kelley: A popular Irish name, it means "lively". It can be a great alternative to "Kelly".

- Kelsi: Originated from Irish, it translates to "brave".

- Kielo: This exotic Finnish name means "lily of the valley".

- Ksenia: it means "hospitable" in Russian.

- Leah: This Biblical name has a Hebrew origin and is gradually becoming a favorite among young parents.

- Louise: The French name translates to "lady warrior".

- Leilani: Originated from Hawaiian, it means "child of heaven".

- Leona: This fierce name means "lion" in French.

- Liana: It translates to "lily" from French.

- Lyra: this unique name means "lyrical" in Greek.

- Leyla: An Arabic word, it means "born at night time".

- Lalita: Derived from Sanskrit, it means "pleasant" or "kind".

- Lana: A poetic name, it has been derived from Irish and means "a little rock".

- Lapis: The name was given to the azure-blue shade which is quite popular in fashion.

- Latasha: It means "joyful" in English.

- Laveda: Originated from Latin, it means "purified".

- Leal: Derived from African, it means "faithful".

- Lera: In Spanish, it is often related to the Virgin Mary. Needless to say, it would be an instant choice for all the Biblical fans.

- Leysa: Derived from Ukrainian, it means "defender of mankind".

- Lilja: The Finnish version of "lily".

- Lina: It means "tender" in Arabic.

- Liv: It means "life" in Norse.

- Melody: If you want your daughter to be a musician, then nothing can be better than this Greek originated name which means "song" or "rhythm".

- Maureen: Maureen is the Irish version of Mary.

- Melina: It means "honey" in Greek.

- Mable: It means "lovable" in English.

- Mada: The Arabic word translates to a "path".

- Maha: in African, Maha translates to "the girl with beautiful eyes".

- Mahta: It has been originated from Persian and means "moonlight".

- Maisi: It translates to "pearl" in Irish and can be spelled as "Maisie" as well.

- Maitea: The Spanish originated name translates to "love".

- Maja: The Swedish version of "pearl".

- Malvinia: The Latin name translates to "tender" and "soft".

- Margain: In Armenian, it means "pearl".

- Marlowe: It English, it means "the one who came from the hills".

- Marsali: It's the Gaelic version of "pearl".

- Marvina: It has been originated from Celtic and means "from the sea".

- Mavis: The name is associated with the famous bird and has a French origin.

- Maya: It has a Hindu origin and is associated with "force" and "mystery". It is also a name given to one of the major Hindu goddesses.

- Maysan: In Arabic, a "bright" star is known as Maysan.

- Meena: It has a Sanskrit origin and translates to "a precious stone".

- Melika: The word has multiple meanings. In Hindi, the name is given to a mystical nymph while in Persian it translates to "a plant".

- Michie: It has a Japanese origin and means "graceful flower".

- Milja: In Finnish, it means "freeborn".

- Miya: It translates to "beauty" from Japanese.

- Morise: The Hebrew origin name literally translates to the phrase "god teaches".

- Naomi: Originally a Biblical name, there is just something about "Naomi" that is too chic and stylish, which makes it such a hit.

- Nadia: It means "hope" in Russian. Its French version is "Nadine", which is also a good choice.

- Nayeli: The Arabic name translates to "grace".

- Nessa: It means "pure" in Greek.

- Naida: The name was given to water nymphs in Greek mythology.

- Nada: The Arabic name translates to "dew".

- Nadege: It has been originated from Slavic and translates to "hope".

- Naiara: This Spanish originated name is associated with the Virgin Mary.

- Najla: It means "star" in Arabic.

- Nakeish: Originated from African, it literally translates to "her life".

- Nanelle: It has a Hebrew origin and means "grace".

- Napia: It has a Latin origin and means "of the valley".

- Nazima: The Arabic name translates to "breeze".

- Naveena: Originated from Native American, it translates to "new".

- Nawa: If you are a nature lover, then you can go ahead with this Egyptian name. It translates to "storm".

- Neela: A Sanskrit word, which is often used as a name as well. It translates to "sky blue" or simply "blue".

- Nella: It means "light" in Greek.

- Nerine: In Greek mythology, the term is given to "sea nymphs".

- Nissa: The Scandinavian name means "friendly".

- Nizana: It means "blossom" in Hebrew.

- Noma: Originated from Norse, it means "fate".

- Norine: This Latin word translates to "honor".

- Nysa: It translates to "goal" in Greek.

- Ophelia: Get inspired from the famous Shakespeare play (Hamlet) and give your little one this legendary name.

- Oriana: It means "golden" in Latin.

- Oprah: Name her after one of the most famous female stars in the world. It is a Hebrew name and translates to "fawn".

- Oriel: The French name translates to "bird".

- Odelia: It means "wealthy" in French.

- Olena: French originated name which translates to "gold".

- Osyka: The Native American name is given to an "eagle".

- Pandora: A universally known name, it means "all gifted" in Greek.

- Priscilla: The Latin name translates to "ancient".

- Pia: Short yet meaningful, it means "pious" in Latin.

- Petra: Originated from German, it means "rock".

- Pazice: The Hebrew originated name translates to "gold".

- Pegeen: It means "pearl" in Greek.

- Primrose: A beautiful flower.

- Quies: Derived from Latin, it means "restful".

- Robin: The fun and sparkly name of the bird, it also means "bright" in English.

- Rosemary: In Latin, it means "dew of the sea".

- Ramona: A Spanish name, it translates to "a wise defender".

- Rosalie: The Italian version of "Rose".
- Rhiannon: A poetic choice, it has been derived from Welsh, and means "a great queen".
- Raven: The black bird, which is considered auspicious in many religions.
- Regan: From the Shakespeare's play (King Lear).
- Riva: It stands for the phrase "regain strength" in Latin.
- Reine: It means "queen" in French.
- Rabea: It symbolizes "spring" in Arabic.
- Rafa: The Arabic word translates to "happy".
- Rahele: Taken from Persian, it means "traveler".
- Ranit: In Hebrew, it means "my song".
- Rena: Originated from Greek, it means "peace".
- Rohais: In French, it means the one who is brave.
- Sahe: Short yet modest, this is one such name that would be an instant favorite among your loved ones. It means "wise" in English. It is also the name of the popular spice.
- Shiloh: One of the most unique Biblical names of all, it was the name given to one of the prophets.
- Stella: It translates to "star" in both Latin and Swedish.
- Sasha: An authentic Russian name, it translates to "defender of humanity". The name was originally given to Alexander and was a common choice for a boy's name. Though, it gradually became popular worldwide and is now opted as a girl name as well.

- Sabrina: Sabrina was originally the name given to a Celtic goddess. Though, with time and several fairytale stories, the name has become synonymous to something dreamy and magical.

- Shannon: In Irish, it means "old" and "wise".

- Sharon: Derived from Hebrew, it means a "field".

- Skylar: The Egyptian version of "sky", it can come out as a popular unisex name as well.

- Suri: In Persian, the name is depicted to a "red rose".

- Serena: It is the Latin version of "serene".

- Scout: A Native American name which means "to listen". The name became quite popular with the release of the novel, To Kill a Mockingbird.

- Sonnet: The word is given to describe a lyrical poem. It has been originated from Italian.

- Sheena: A Gaelic word, it translates to "a gift from the god".

- Salome: A name with an exotic pronunciation, it means "peaceful" in Hebrew. The same meaning can be derived from the word "Salma".

- Sapphire: One of the rarest gemstones in the world, having a distinctive blue shade. If your daughter has blue eyes, then the name would be matched flawlessly.

- Soraya: A Persian name given to one of the brightest constellations in the sky.

- Shea: Short yet meaningful, it means "bright" in Irish.

- Sloan: Derived from Scottish, it means "warrior".

  - Sabra: In Arabic, it means "patience".

- Sabah: The name has an Arabic origin and translates to "morning".

- Sadbh: An exotic Irish name, it means "sweet".

- Sadira: Originated from Arabic, it means "end of the valley".

- Sahar: In Arabic, Sahar is translated to "awakening".

- Saki: Short yet poignant, the name has a Japanese origin and translates to "cape".

- Sakura: One of the most renowned Japanese names, it is both thoughtful and bubbly. It translates to "cherry blossom".

- Sana: An Arabic name which can be translated to different words, such as "bright", "radiance", or "splendor".

- Sanjna: In Hindu mythology, the name was given to the wife of the Sun. It can also be spelled as "Sanjana".

- Sarita: The name has multiple meanings. In Spanish, Sarita translates to "Little Sarah", while in Hindi, it means "princess".

- Satu: This short yet beautiful word translates to "fairy tale" in Finnish.

- Sawni: A unique Native American name, it translates to "echo" and definitely has a peculiar ring to it.

- Sekhet: It has been derived from Egyptian and literally translates to the phrase "to be powerful".

- Sena: In Latin, Sena was the goddess of the moon.

- Shakti: Shakti is one of the many names of the major Hindu goddess Durga.

- Sian: Originated from Welsh, it translates to the phrase "God is greatest".

- Sidera: This unique name has been originated from Latin and translates to "like a moon" or "luminous".

- Sima: Short but thoughtful, it has multiple meanings. In Scottish, it translates to "listener", while in Persian it means "face".

- Silver: There is nothing more special than naming your little one after the precious metal.

- Sinead: Originated from Irish, it means "a gift from the god". It can also be spelled as "Sineaid".

- Siv: One of the prominent names of Norse origin, it was the name given to Thor's wife.

- Sofiya: Sofiya can be a great alternative to "Sofia". It has been originated from Ukrainian and means "wisdom".

- Solon: In Greek, it means "wise".

- Soma: The name translates to "moon" in Hindi.

- Suma: A name given to a flower in Hindi.

- Syllis: Syllis was one of the most powerful nymphs in Greek mythology.

- Tara: The name has multiple meanings. In Irish, it stands for a "tree", whereas in Hindi, it means a "star".

- Tamara: A lights and breezy name that will certainly be loved by all. It has a Hebrew origin and translates to "palm tree".

- Talia: Originated from Hebrew, it means "dew from heaven".

    - Tabitha: An Arabic name, it translated to "gazelle".

- Tori: A futuristic name, it actually has a Norse origin and translates to "Thor's spear".

- Thea: It means "melting ice" in English.

- Tianna: The Swedish name translates to "victor".

- Trina: The name has a Celtic origin and translates to "wise".

- Trish: It means "traveler" in English.

- Tia: Short yet meaningful, this Norse originated name literally translates to "Thor's stone".

- Tulia: Originated from Greek, it means "God's gift".

- Trishna: The name certainly has a ring to it. It means "teacher".

- Tandy: A Native American name, it means "a flower".

- Taika: A Finnish name, it means "magic".

- Tala: Short yet poignant, this Native American name stands for "wolf".

- Tamala: An African originated name, it means "tree".

- Tana: The name was given to the fire goddess in Greek.

- Tayen: One of the most poignant Native American names, it translates to "new moon".

- Teah: It means "goddess" in Greek.

- Tesia: A Greek originated name, it is translated to the phrase "Loved by God".

- Thema: A Greek goddess.

- Treasa: Originated from Welsh, it means "fair town".

- Tuulia: In Norse, it is translated to "thunder".
- Tyra: This exotic name translates to "river".
- Tzuriya: It means "bird" in Hebrew.
- Uma: It means "the second daughter" in Nigerian and "crescent moon" in Hindi.
- Uli: A Teutonic name, it translates to "from a noble land".
- Urbi: A Greek name, it means "heavenly".
- Violet: Besides the beautiful color, it means "happy girl" in Hindi.
- Venus: One of the major planets in our solar system and a Roman goddess, who is associated with beauty and feminine traits.
- Valentina: Derived from Latin, it translates to "strong".
- Viviana: It means "victory" in Latin.
- Vanya: It has multiple meanings. In Green, it means "butterfly", whereas in Hebrew, it means "god's gift".
- Varna: The German term can be translated to "sacred wisdom".
- Vianne: This beautiful name has been originated from Latin and means "evening star".
- Viera: A fierce name, it has been originated from Norse and translates to "a female warrior".
- Venetia: A German name, it is associated with bravery.
- Verena: A common Dutch name, it can be translated to "from the bridge".

- Valdis: A unique name it has been originated from Welsh and means "the chosen one".

- Valen: A Teutonic name, it is associated with the one who is spiritual.

- Varinka: It means "rose" in Hebrew.

- Varsha: This beautiful name translates to "rain" in Hindi.

- Willow: This would be chosen by every nature lover. The popular name is originally given to a beautiful tree.

- Wallis: The name has been derived from Egyptian and means "newly born".

- Wangari: This German name certainly has a ring to it. It means "wanderer", which makes it quite poetic.

- Wyn: Short and bubbly, this English name means "from the farm".

- Xiomara: A meaningful Greek name, it means "welcoming". The name is definitely making a comeback these days.

- Xena: If you think your daughter can carry this legendary name, then there is nothing wrong in naming her after the famous warrior.

- Xyliana: Originated from German, it means "famous".

- Xylona: This Greek originated name translates to "the one who lives in the forest".

- Yasmin: Originated from Turkish, it is a common alternative to the famous name "Jasmine". It can also be spelled as "Yasmine".

- Yara: Yara is one of those names, which has a peculiar ring to it. It was originally given to Brazilian goddess with green hair.

- Yulia: A common English surname, it is now being used as a name. It means "from the yew tree valley".

- Yana: The Russian variant of "Helen".

- Yona: A Native American name, it translates to "rain" in English.

- Yuliya: Originated from Norse, it would be adored by all the Christmas lovers. It means "born during the Yuletide".

- Zara: A popular Arabic name, it means "princess".

- Zephyr: The Greek originated name literally means "lifespan of Zeus".

- Zahra: The Hebrew word translates to "dawn".

- Zola: Originated from African, it means "life".

- Zora: It means "alive" in Greek.

- Zooey: Fun and bubbly, the name means "life" in Greek.

- Zelena: In Hebrew, it means "protector".

- Zarah: Originate from Arabic, it means "father's ornament".

- Zayda: This Hebrew word, means "beautiful princess".

- Zayna: This Polish word literally translates to the phrase "God protect the king" and has a Biblical association.

- Ziva: This thoughtful name means "free" in Teutonic.

- Zoya: Originated from Slavic, it means "dawn".

We are sure that by now, you must be able to come up with a perfect name for your little one! If you are still not sure, then turn the page and be inspired by some of the most prominent names that are famous in different parts of the world. Go international and make your little one stand out from the crowd.

Chapter 8 – The Most Beautiful Names Around The World

These days parents would like to leave no stone unturned in order to come up with just the perfect name for their baby. Chuck the age-old phenomenon of picking a commonly used name and walk a few extra miles to come up with the kind of name that will leave everyone impressed.

Why not take inspiration from various cultures and know how babies are named in different parts of the world. We have come up with a comprehensive list of some of the most beautiful names of babies that are used all over the world. With the listing of various names, we have mentioned their meaning and the origin of the word, so that you would have a better idea about the name. If you like one of these names, then research a little and unravel its true meaning. You never know, you might end up commencing a revolution in its own way by giving your baby the name that they will absolutely love for the rest of their lives!

- Aapeli: Breathe (Finnish origin)
- Abir: Fragrant or essence (Arabic origin)
- Abisha: Gift of god (Hebrew origin)
- Ailin: Noble or thoughtful (Irish origin)
- Alva: Sublime; the one with high moral ethics (Arabic origin)
- Alvy: Olive (Irish origin)
- Amare: The one who possesses great strength (African origin)

- Bastet: The famous Egyptian cat-goddess (Egyptian origin)

- Bellamy: A handsome friend (French origin)

- Bevin: A young and handsome soldier (Celtic origin)

- Bifrost: A bridge that leads from the Earth to Asgard (Norse origin)

- Binah: A talented dancer (African origin)

- Blair: A child of the fields and the meadows (Scottish origin)

- Bo: Something precious (Chinese origin); Commanding (Danish origin)

- Breandan: Prince or royal (Celtic origin)

- Bryce: Son of a noble person (Latin origin)

- Callahan: A beautiful conflict or strive (Irish origin)

- Canan: A beloved person (Turkish origin)

- Carlin: A champion (Irish origin)

- Cassidy: Curly-headed or someone who is clever (Gaelic origin)

- Chakra: The circle of life, or the symbol of the sun (Hindu origin)

- Charybdis: A whirlpool; Daughter of Poseidon (Green origin)

- Chaska: First born child, usually a son (Native American origin)

- Cyan: Blue-greenish color (Multiple origins)

- Dael: A small village (Dutch origin)
- Darby: A free and independent person (Norse origin)
- Darcy: River (Irish origin)
- Derya: A deep ocean (Turkish origin)
- Devi: A goddess (Hindu origin)
- Eero: An eternal ruler or king (Finnish origin)
- Eisa: Jesus (Arabic origin)
- Ekon: Something strange or outlandish, yet positive (African origin)
- Elgin: The one who is noble and kind (Celtic origin)
- Elia: Answer to your prayers (Spanish origin)
- Enar: Fighter or a warrior (Norse origin)
- Errol: The one who is noble (Latin origin)
- Evin: Swift and fast (Irish origin)
- Fay: Commonly used to call a raven (Latin origin)
- Forba: Strong and caring (Scottish origin)
- Frici: An everlasting ruler or king (Teutonic origin)
- Ganya: The garden of the God (Hebrew origin)
- Garuda: An exotic bird who carried the Lord Vishnu (Hindu origin)
- Gili: Joy and eternal happiness (Hebrew origin)
- Gretel: Pearl or white as a pearl (German origin)

- Gwyn: Blessed with all the joy and happiness (Welsh origin)

- Helge: Sacred or blessed (Norse origin)

- Icarus/Icarius: Commonly known as the Athenian legend that learned to fly. (Greek origin)

- Ida: Perseverant and hard-working (German origin)

- Iman: Faith or kindness (Arabic origin)

- Indra: Ruler of all the other gods (Hindu origin)

- Jude: Young and dynamic (Latin origin)

- Kala: Princess (Hawaiian origin); God of time (Hindu origin)

- Kalani: The sky (Hawaiian origin)

- Kami: A divine and enigmatic aura (Japanese origin)

- Karel: Strong and independent (Czech origin)

- Karin: Pure (Swedish origin); Soulmate or companion (Arabic origin)

- Lenci: Light or a source of light (Greek origin)

- Leonce: Lion or fierce (French origin)

- Lin: Forest or a beautiful place in the wild (Chinese origin)

- Malin: Above or from the tower (Swedish origin)

- Margo: Pearl; a common variant of Margaret (Hungarian origin)

- Mariam: Variant of Mother Mary (Arabic origin)

- Marquise: Someone who is either royal or belongs to the royal family (French origin)
- Meredith: Protector or a chief (Welsh origin)
- Merrill: A person who is famous and renowned (Teutonic origin)
- Mika: A gift from the God (Hebrew origin)
- Mischa: Someone who is nothing less than a lord (Russian origin)
- Mosi: First born child (Egyptian origin)
- Neci: Intense and thoughtful (Latin origin)
- Nikita: The one that can't be conquered (Russian origin); Earth (Hindu origin)
- Noe: Misty (Hawaiian origin)
- Nour: Luminous or source of light (Egyptian origin)
- Oriel: A beautiful bird, commonly known for its orange markings (French origin)
- Ove: Ancestors; something old (Norse origin)
- Palash: Blooming tree (Hindu origin)
- Pax: Peace, also denoted for the Roman goddess (Latin origin)
- Paz: Gold or golden (Hebrew origin); Peace (Spanish origin)
- Pili: The second born (Egyptian origin)
- Quillan: The small one or cub (Gaelic origin)
- Pegasus: The renowned winged horse (Greek origin)

- Ra: The sun god of Heliopolis (Egyptian origin)
- Raine: The strong one (Teutonic origin)
- Ram: The supreme god (Hindu origin)
- Rashida: The one who is always right (Egyptian origin)
- Reaghan: Noble and kind (Celtic origin)
- Rene: To rise again or reborn (French origin)
- Rio: River (Spanish origin)
- Sabra: Patience or thoughtfulness (Arabic origin)
- Shanahan: Wise and intelligent (Irish origin)
- Sheridan: The one who can't be tamed (Celtic origin)
- Shiv: One of the primary Hindu Gods (Hindu origin)
- Siv: Wife of Thor; The peaceful defender (Norse origin)
- Soma: Moon (Hindu origin); Horn (Hungarian origin)
- Suzu: The one who would live for a long time (Japanese origin)
- Tapio: The god of the forest (Finnish origin)
- Tarafah: The sight or the shimmering of an eye (Arabic origin)
- Vivien: Full of life and joy (Latin origin)
- Zayne: Rose; a friendly visitor (Arabic origin)
- Zooey: Life or full of life (Greek origin)

Those were some really meaningful names, right? We tried to take inspiration from various cultures and geographic locations in order to come up with a list of names that are not only unique or sounds good, but have such a thoughtful meaning behind them as well. From Norse and Greek mythology to Welsh and Teutonic names, our list would certainly let you pick a unique name for your little one.

We are pretty sure that by now, you must have already had a few names in your mind. Before you shortlist them and come up with a selective list of names, be sure to have a look at the kind of names that you should avoid giving your kids in the next chapter.

Chapter 9 – Common Names To Avoid

Naming your baby can be one of the most crucial decisions of your life, knowing that it will not only affect you but the entire life of your little one as well. By now, you must have gotten an idea about naming your baby and how you can come up with an interesting name for them as well. Though, there are a few names that you should avoid using. If you have them on your list, then you should consider scratching them off. We will give a compelling reason for why naming your baby "Adam" or "Logan" is a bad idea. Let's have a look!

1. Adam: We certainly can't start our list with any other name than Adam. This is one of the most commonly used names in the world, which is exactly why you should avoid using it. Yes, the name sounds good and has an amazing meaning to it, but don't be so lethargic. Your kid will always go unnoticed with such a common name. The same goes with other names like William, John, Amy, or Amanda.

2. Breen: The name might sound really good, but it means "sadness". It has an Irish origin and is given to babies who come with sad news. Needless to say, one should always refrain themselves from giving their little one this name.

3. Campbell: Yes, the name definitely sounds good and is opted by hundreds of parents worldwide, but it doesn't come with a positive meaning. The Gaelic origin name means "someone with a crooked mouth" and will always make your kid doubt their physical appearance, which might even cause an emotional turmoil in the long haul.

4. Dick: Needless to say, if you want your son to get bullied or called upon his whole life, then give him a lifelong punishment by naming him "Dick". Just don't do it!

5. Elfie: Naming your little one Elfie might seem like a great plan when they are kids, but what will happen as they grow old. A 40-year old woman with a name like that would certainly be embarrassed almost every single day. No matter how cute your baby is, you can't name them something like that for real. Having a nickname is one thing and actually giving them a name like "Princess" or "Angel" is a big no. Instead, give them the kind of names that would age well.

6. Emily: Another common name with a bad meaning, it translates to "enemy" or "rival" and should definitely be avoided, unless you want your daughter to be your enemy for the rest of her life.

7. Gideon: The name might sound good, but it is used to depict those who have a stump for a hand. The meaning of the name itself makes it a bad choice. Giving your baby such a negative name might affect them drastically in the long run.

8. Jabez: We understand that sometimes childbirth can get a little rough, but if you give your baby this name, then you might have to relive that painful moment for the rest of your life. It means "born out of pain" and can definitely not be the right choice to name your baby.

9. Logan: Yes, it might surprise you, considering the fact that it is such a popular option, but the name comes with a distrustful meaning. It means something which is hollow or someone who has come from a hollow place. Even though the name might seem rugged or could a mainstream one, but you should try to avoid using this one for your kid. Our name reflects our behavior and the course of our entire life, and you certainly would not like to give your baby such a negative name.

10. Ransom: The name has a negative meaning and is often linked to the amount criminals ask while holding hostages. Though it has a cowboy feel, but it should always be avoided. Prefer naming your boy Randy or Randall, as they sound similar to Ransom and have a better meaning.

There are also some other names that you should avoid using like Persephone (the one who brings death), Calvin (bald), Saskia (knife), Cessair (sorrow), Porita (pig), and a lot more. Before you finalize your baby's name, do a little research and be sure that it doesn't have a negative meaning.

Having a cross-language reference is also a good idea. We live in a diverse world where people from different backgrounds come together. A particular name might have a positive meaning in one language but can mean something way too different in another dialect. It is always recommended to cross check everything and take a reference from various languages before coming up with that one final name.

Now, when you know about the kind of names that you should avoid, there is nothing that can stop you anymore. Pick a perfect name for your little one and give them the most adorable present of their life!

Conclusion

Congratulations for completing the book so soon! We are sure you must have had a great time exploring different names and knowing the meaning of so many new words as well.

Naming a baby can sometimes be the hardest job of all. It becomes a part of their identity and represents them for the rest of their lives. Thankfully, we have just made the job a whole lot easier for you. Here, in this guide, we gave you in-depth information about naming your little one.

We started by exploring significant factors that every parent should keep in mind while naming their baby. We also made you learn an interesting way of coming up with a beautiful name for your little one and how you can be inspired by the world around you. A comprehensive list of some of the finest boys, girls, and unisex names was also suggested so that you can handpick a perfect name. To get your inspired with various cultures of the world, we also listed some of the most thoughtful names of babies around the world. Lastly, to help you shortlist a perfect name, we suggested the kind of common names that every parent should avoid.

By now, you must have already handpicked some of your favorite names. Why not research a little and make sure that these names will surpass the passage of time and will make your little one stand out from the crowd. Though, when you are doing so, always listen to your heart. We can suggest you these beautiful names, but only you need to make that final choice. Let your heart decide your baby's name and enjoy this process. It is a once-in-a-lifetime opportunity and you should cherish it to the most!

Copyright 2016 by Casey Robson - All rights reserved.

All rights Reserved. No part of this publication or the information in it may be quoted from or reproduced in any form by means such as printing, scanning, photocopying or otherwise without prior written permission of the copyright holder.

Disclaimer and Terms of Use: Effort has been made to ensure that the information in this book is accurate and complete, however, the author and the publisher do not warrant the accuracy of the information, text and graphics contained within the book due to the rapidly changing nature of science, research, known and unknown facts and internet. The Author and the publisher do not hold any responsibility for errors, omissions or contrary interpretation of the subject matter herein. This book is presented solely for motivational and informational purposes only.

Made in the USA
Middletown, DE
14 September 2017